D0492954

THE
DAILY
PROMISE

THE DAILY PROMISE

100 WAYS TO FEEL HAPPY ABOUT YOUR LIFE

DOMONIQUE BERTOLUCCI

hardie grant books

For Sophia and Tobias

Preface

"The most important relationship in your life is the relationship you have with yourself. Because no matter what happens, you will always be with yourself."

DIANE VON FÜRSTENBERG

People often say to me: 'You seem so happy and cheerful, don't you ever have a bad day?' Of course I do. I wouldn't be human if I didn't. But what I don't do is let the way I feel about my day change the way I feel about myself.

Most people are looking outside themselves for ways to feel good on the inside. The truth is that although they are the only person who can build their confidence up, the way they think and act is doing nothing but tear it down.

If there is anything I've learned in my forty-something years it's that nobody else can make me feel good or bad about myself. It is up to me to decide how I want to feel and I've decided that, regardless of the details at any given time, I'm going to feel good.

I was a naturally confident child but, like everyone else, my life has had its share of ups and downs, celebrations and cruel blows.

One of the most formative of these came when I was ten years old. During that year I moved to a new school and was subjected to a campaign of bullying that still has the power to reduce me to tears. Way back then, I made a decision about the impact I would let this experience have on me. Despite the vile things this bully was saying and doing, deep down I knew I was a good person. If she couldn't see it that was her problem but I wasn't going to allow her false perspective to alter my own views about myself.

I decided to feel good about myself.

This decision has stood me in good stead throughout my life. It gave me the courage to stand up for myself the next time I was bullied—this time at work. It motivated me to end a relationship that many said I should stay in but that I knew wasn't right for me and it fuelled me with the energy I needed to walk away from a high-flying career and follow the road that led me here today.

My decision ensured that a series of painful miscarriages, each one breaking my heart, never broke my spirit and it has continued to carry me through the disappointments and setbacks that come with any life well lived.

Way back then, I made a promise to myself. I promised I would always do what I had to do to feel good about who I was and the life I lived. I knew this was my responsibility; I would never let anyone bring me down and I wouldn't wait for someone else to make me feel good either. And I was going to take this responsibility seriously.

All these years later, I still do.

When I wrote *The Kindness Pact*, I wanted to explain why it was so important to be kind to yourself; to treat yourself with love and respect. How by doing so you would build your confidence, nurture your self-esteem and have more energy to do what you want to do and be who you want to be.

This book invites you to put the *Pact* into action by making a series of promises to yourself. Over time these daily commitments will create a fundamental shift in the way you feel about you and your life.

You could sit down and read this book from cover to cover but its greatest gift is as a daily guide. Choose one page each day and put that promise into action. It doesn't matter if you do this in sequence or choose a random page. What matters is that you do it and keep doing it until the promises described become the way you truly feel.

You deserve to feel good about who you are and the life you live. Make that your promise today.

If you would like to learn more about getting the life you want and loving the life you've got, you can sign up for my free training course *Life: make the most of yours*, download *The Kindness Pact Workbook* and access a range of other free resources at domoniquebertolucci.com.

You can download *The Daily Promise* app from the iPhone app store and get your *Daily Promise* delivered direct to your phone.

The Eight Promises

Feeling good about who you are and the life you live shouldn't depend on a specific outcome, yet all too often I hear people put themselves down or beat themselves up because they haven't done this or got that. Your confidence shouldn't be dependent on the goals you have achieved, nor should it be dependent on the feedback you get from others, your dress size or the amount in your bank account. But if your self-confidence isn't based on what you've got or what you've done, how do you build and maintain it?

The answer is simple. Make the commitment to treat yourself with the same kindness you show the most important people in your life.

The key to feeling good about who you are and the life you live is built on this pact – the **Eight Promises**. Each affirmation in this book represents a different promise and explains the role it plays in building and maintaining your confidence and self-belief.

When you commit to the **Eight Promises**, your life you will no longer be burdened with anxiety, doubt or insecurity and instead you will feel good about who you are and the life you live.

The First Promise: Accept your imperfections
I am perfectly imperfect.

There is no such thing as perfection and yet so many people exhaust themselves and erode their confidence in the pursuit of it. When you accept your imperfections, you acknowledge that, like everyone else, you have many positive qualities but that you also have other, less positive ones … and that's okay.

Once you have released yourself from the burden of perfectionism, you are free to use your positive qualities to their fullest. You can also decide which of your less-than-ideal qualities you would like to invest your energy in improving and which qualities everyone else will need to accept as 'part of the parcel'.

The Second Promise: Always do your best

I always do my best and my best is always good enough.

When you set impossible goals that you have no real chance of achieving, you are setting yourself up for failure; when you promise to always do your best you are able to have much more realistic expectations of yourself. Your sense of self-worth will no longer be dependent on outcomes and you will feel good about who you are regardless of what you have or haven't been able to achieve.

When you truly believe your best is good enough, you can accept that you are having a bad day, or feeling a bit ordinary, without this affecting the way you feel about yourself.

The Third Promise: Stop comparing yourself

I have no need to see myself as more or less than anyone else.

Comparing yourself to others will always leave you feeling inadequate. Even if you find yourself thinking that you are superior in some way, this will only give your self-esteem a short-term boost.

When you stop comparing yourself to others, the only person you will need to impress is yourself. You will be able to source your confidence from within and it will no longer be affected by anything anyone else says, does or has.

The Fourth Promise: Believe in your potential

I fully expect my life to be happy and rewarding.

Not only is worrying a big waste of energy, it also sends a clear message to your subconscious about your expectations in life. Instead of worrying about things that might never happen, when you believe in your potential, you are able to focus your attention and your efforts on making the things you *do* want your reality.

You don't have to be in denial about potential negative outcomes, but once you've acknowledged your fears, you are able to put them to the side and continue on towards the happy and rewarding future you know you deserve.

The Fifth Promise: Silence your inner critic

I only welcome thoughts that support and encourage me.

You are the guardian of your self-esteem. If you speak to yourself in a harsh, critical or belittling way, your confidence will wither, but if you never speak to yourself more harshly than you would to a small child, you will nurture your confidence and allow your self-esteem to flourish.

Changing the way you think takes practice, but while at first you might not be able to control every thought you have, you will always be able to decide which ones you want to pay attention to.

The Sixth Promise: Challenge yourself

I am brave and willing to step outside of my comfort zone.

Confidence and self-belief are like muscles; you need to exercise them if you want them to grow stronger. One of the best ways to build these muscles is by stepping outside of your comfort zone. When you challenge yourself, you are telling your subconscious that you believe in yourself and that you are willing to back yourself in new circumstances and situations.

When you step outside of your comfort zone, take on a challenge or learn something new, you open yourself up to the added confidence boost of discovering that you are actually not so bad at something you never knew you could do.

The Seventh Promise: Stop making excuses

I take full responsibility for who I am and the life I lead.

Nobody is living the perfect life. What some people are better at than others is living their best life. If you are not living your best life, you need to examine not only the things that are getting in your way, but the reasons why you are letting them.

When you stop making excuses and start taking responsibility, you are able to enjoy the things that are great about your life, while harbouring no illusions about what you need to change if you are to enjoy everything else.

The Eighth Promise: Love yourself

I always treat myself with love and respect.

If you want to feel good about who you are and the life you live, you need to make building your confidence and your self-belief a high priority.

Love yourself. Treat yourself with as much love and respect as you would your closest friend, be understanding and forgiving of your failings and, above all, be as kind to yourself as you are to the other important people in your life.

You deserve to feel good
about who you are and the life you live.

I love my life

Living a life you love is not a lofty goal or something that happens to other people.

You deserve a happy and fulfilling life. Don't let anyone tell you otherwise.

Confidence comes from within.

I am confident

Nobody else can make you feel confident.

You will never find confidence if you look for it outside of yourself. The only person who can build your confidence is you. Make sure nothing you do tears it down.

You are the guardian of your self-esteem.
Guard it vigilantly.

I protect my self-esteem

When you are a child, the adults in your life are responsible for protecting your self-esteem and helping your confidence to grow.

As an adult the only person who can do this is you. Do it well.

Perfection is an unachievable goal.
Nobody can be perfect … not even you.

I accept my imperfections

There's no such thing as a perfect person so don't even try.

Instead of making yourself miserable trying to be perfect, enjoy your life and accept that you are perfectly imperfect.

There is a big difference between doing your best and needing to be the best.

I strive for excellence

Needing to be the best is a very risky strategy if you also want to be happy.

Every time you set out to be the best you also run the risk of being the worst. Instead of trying to be better than someone else, redirect your energy towards being the very best version of yourself.

There is no upside to comparing yourself
to others,
only the downside of watching your confidence
disappear.

I am equal

Never compare yourself to someone else.

When you play the comparison game, your faults don't lie in the things you see as missing or lacking about you. Your only true fault was comparing yourself to someone else in the first place.

If you can do something about it, do it.
If you can't, let it go.

I am at peace with myself

Don't waste time or energy worrying about things over which you have no control.

When something is bothering you, take a moment to evaluate the situation. Choose to take action or find acceptance; then get on with the rest of your life.

*Never speak to yourself more harshly
than you would to a small child.*

I speak kindly to myself

Most people speak to themselves using a tone or language they would never dream of using for anyone else.

Protect your self-esteem by speaking to yourself with the same kindness, love and respect you use when speaking to the other important people in your life.

Learn to believe in yourself
the way a child does …
Unconditionally.

I believe in myself

When you think about doing something, make sure doubting yourself is not your first step.

Start by believing in yourself without question. Once you have convinced yourself that anything is possible, you can then start to examine the things you will need to do to *actually* make it possible.

You don't need to be cruel to be kind,
but you do need to be honest.

I am honest with myself

Don't be in denial about how things are and how you would like them to be.

It is only when you are truly honest with yourself, even about the more unpleasant or uncomfortable truths, that you can start to create your best possible life.

The better you take care of yourself,
the better you are able to take care of the other
important people in your life.

I take care of myself

Make time each day to do something just for you.

This doesn't need to be something big, expensive or particularly time consuming. Just do something that reminds you that you are important too.

It is no less unreasonable
to expect yourself to be perfect
than it is to expect perfection
from the people you love.

I treat myself with kindness

When you make a mistake, don't compound it by beating yourself up.

Forgive yourself for falling down and use the same encouraging and supportive words you would offer a friend to help you get back up.

Discovering room for improvement
doesn't mean you didn't do your best.
It just means that next time
your best will be even better.

I celebrate my efforts

Every time you complete something you
will always see ways you can improve it next
time.

Don't let this recognition of how you
could do better tomorrow distract you from
acknowledging the effort you have already
made to get to where you are today.

In life there is always the good stuff
and then there is the rest of it.

I am resilient

Regardless of how it may look from afar, everyone's life contains ups, downs and a whole lot of in-between.

The mark of a happy life is not that it always runs smoothly—it's how easily you are able to navigate your way around the bumps in the road.

Being prepared is the best investment
you can make in your future.

I prepare for the future

There's no point worrying about what tomorrow might bring.

A far smarter course of action is to make a plan, set a goal and do what it takes to give yourself the best chance of having your future unfold the way you want it to.

Become your own best friend.

I support and encourage myself

Don't wait for someone else to boost you up, encourage you or make you feel good about yourself.

Instead of looking outside yourself for ways to feel good on the inside, take responsibility for your self-esteem and become your own best friend.

Stop saying 'I can't'.
You can … if you want to.

I own my choices

So often when people say 'I can't', what they really mean is, 'I don't want to', 'I'm not ready to' or 'I'm afraid to'.

If you don't want to do something, don't do it but instead of undermining your confidence by saying 'I can't', be honest with yourself about the real reasons why.

*Be realistic about what you intend to do
and honest about what you are able to do.*

7th

I respect my boundaries

It is easy to fall into the habit of being a people pleaser—saying yes to everything regardless of whether you want to or not.

Instead of finding yourself in situations where you are desperately looking for ways to get out of your commitments, put clear boundaries in place so you know in advance which requests you are able to accept and which ones you need to firmly decline.

Prioritising your needs doesn't make you selfish,
it makes you self-ist.

I prioritise my needs

These days we all play myriad roles in our lives but in amongst the busyness that this creates, it can be easy to forget yourself and what you need.

Avoid the exhaustion and resentment this can create by making your 'self' one of your most important priorities.

Learn to accept your flaws
with love and grace.

I accept flaws

If you find yourself being critical of the things that are less than perfect about yourself, stop and reframe your thoughts.

Instead of thinking that these things are stopping you from being perfect, remind yourself that, like a diamond, your flaws are intrinsic to who you are.

Don't be intimidated
by someone else's achievements.
Do your best and don't worry about the rest.

I follow my own path

There is a big difference between being impressed by someone else's achievements and being depressed by it.

Everyone progresses through life at their own pace and just because someone gets to where you want to be before you doesn't mean they're better than you. Stay committed to your dreams and know that your time will come.

*Remember, there is always
more to the picture.*

I am generous

Never judge someone as better or worse than you.

Be generous in your assessment. You never know what someone is going through, what challenges they are facing or what heartache and difficulties they are hiding behind the scenes.

Worry is not a sign of love.
It is a symptom of fear.

I make the most of life

No matter how much you love or care about someone, worrying won't keep them safe from harm.

Instead of fretting about what might happen, spend quality time with your loved ones, making the most of the moment that *is* happening.

Your inner dialogue is based on fiction.
It's time to rewrite the story.

I choose positive thoughts

Don't accept your subconscious thoughts
as facts. They're not. Most of your inner
dialogue is nonsense fuelled by your fears
and insecurities.

Stop listening to thoughts that don't
support you and instead reprogram your
subconscious with ideas and affirmations
that do.

There is no such thing
as a good or bad feeling.
All that matters is
the power you give them.

I embrace my feelings

Regardless of how you are feeling, don't try to deny or judge your emotions.

Not all feelings will be enjoyable. Some will be uncomfortable, unpleasant or inconvenient. It is okay to experience them all, just don't let them stand in your way.

When you commit to yourself
and your intentions,
the message you send yourself is
'I am worth this effort'.

I honour my commitments

Don't say yes to something unless you mean it.

Although in the moment you might tell yourself it doesn't matter, failing to do what you say you are going to do, however insignificant, tells your subconscious that failure is a comfortable state for you.

Asking for help is a sign of strength,
not weakness.

I ask for help
when I need it

You can't do it all on your own.

Whether it's a challenge at work, a busy life at home or an audacious goal you want to achieve don't wait until you become overwhelmed. Ask for assistance before you are desperate and become all the stronger for it.

You are good enough,
just as you are.

I like myself

Just because there are things about yourself that you would like to improve doesn't mean that there is anything wrong with you as you are.

Remind yourself, you are good enough, exactly as you are.

Don't set yourself up for failure
before you even begin.

I am optimistic

Instead of being blindly positive, be optimistic.

Whether your goals are for your work, health or life in general, don't set yourself up for failure before you begin by being unreasonable in your expectations.

Expect the best but do so while considering the constraints you face in your day-to-day life.

*Comparing yourself to a celebrity
is no different to comparing yourself
to any other fictional character.*

3rd

I know what I want

When it comes to designing your best life, don't compare yourself to someone you know or, worse, someone you've read about.

Design your own best life. Work out what you really want and need and then make the commitment to making that your reality.

Don't worry about what everyone else thinks.
Have confidence in your ability
to make the right decision for you.

I trust my wisdom

Canvassing other people for their opinion undermines your confidence in your own.

The majority of the time, when you ask a question, you already know the answer. You might not like your answer or wish it was something different but deep within, you already know what is right for you.

If you want to feel like a winner,
you need to learn how to cheer yourself on.

I am my own biggest fan

Learn to cheer yourself on regardless of whether you feel like you are winning or losing.

Knowing that someone believes in you will help you make it to the finish line even if that person is you.

When you challenge yourself,
you send a strong message to your subconscious.
You are saying, 'I am worth the risk'.

I am brave

You don't need to jump out of plane or climb the highest mountain to challenge yourself. Anything that takes you out of your comfort zone will have a very positive effect on your self-esteem.

Be brave. Start with a small challenge and watch your self-confidence soar.

*Taking responsibility for your life
is liberating.*

I get out of my way

Don't wait for someone or something: a job, a partner, a family, a million dollars to make your life okay. Nothing will give you happiness and no one can take it away.

The only thing really standing in the way of your happiness is you.

*Focus on your values
and let everything else fall into place.*

I know what's important

Take the time to work out what matters most to you in life.

When you know what your values are, your priorities will be clear, decision making will be easy and you will find it easier to live a happier and more fulfilling life.

Perfectionism and self-confidence
cannot coexist.

I always do my best

Perfection is impossible.

If you try to be perfect at everything, not only will you fail, you will leave yourself feeling stressed, insecure and inadequate.

If you want to live a happy life, be the best you can be instead.

If you try to do the impossible,
it will be impossible to succeed.

I expect to succeed

There is nothing wrong with wanting your day to flow and your life to run smoothly.

Setting yourself up for success doesn't mean that you are complacent or denying your potential. It means you are wise and not trying to do the impossible.

Comparing yourself to someone else
won't make you feel good about yourself.

I feel good about who I am

Comparing yourself to other people to see how you measure up is a destructive habit; sometimes you'll come out on top and at other times, sadly lacking.

Nothing anyone else does will matter when you learn to base your sense of self on who you are, not what you've done or got.

*One of the most powerful questions
you can ask yourself is
'What will I do differently next time?'*

I am always improving

Every time you do something, as soon as you have finished, you will see ways you could have made it better.

Rather than dwelling on these observations and thinking of them as mistakes, store them in your memory as enhancements for the future.

You are an amazing person,
a complex mix of qualities and
characteristics unique to you.
There is nobody else in the world
quite like you.

I celebrate my uniqueness

Don't apologise to yourself or anyone else
for the quirks that make up your personality.
    It is your unique mix of qualities that set
you apart from everyone else.

If you don't change anything,
nothing changes.

I see the way forward

Nothing will change unless you change. The same thinking that got you to where you are won't get you to where you want to go.

If you want to get a different result, start by thinking about your challenge in a different way. You will soon know what you need to do to make your new updated vision your reality.

Nobody's life is perfect.
What looks like perfection from
afar is usually the result of hard work
and commitment.

I work for what I want

It's easy to look at someone else's life
and think that it must be easier for them.
Everyone's life is different and chances
are that whoever you are envying, they are
envying someone else themselves.

Instead of wondering 'if only' or wishing
your life away, work with what you have
and make the commitment to your best
life today.

Gratitude for what you have
is one of the greatest gifts you can give yourself.

I am thankful for the life I live

Most people spend far more energy thinking about what they want and don't have than they ever spend thinking about what they do.

Instead of focusing on what is missing from your life, enjoy your life for what it already is.

*Decide what you want to be brilliant at
and be okay with just being okay at the rest.*

I am brilliant

Life is not like a classroom where the grades you earn for each subject are consolidated and used to guide your future.

Take control of your life by deciding when you want to score an 'A' and when a pass mark will be more than good enough.

*Be realistic about your resources
and do the best you can with what you've got.*

I use my energy wisely

Doing your best doesn't mean you have to be brilliant at everything all of the time.

Consider the other commitments and priorities in your life and decide what your best needs to be in each individual situation.

Don't believe everything you read, see or hear.
It's usually only a small slice of the truth.

I am the source of my confidence

Don't chase a false reality.

Celebrities, reality stars, people on social media and even your friends are all only sharing a small part of their lives—the part they want you to see.

If you want to feel good about your life, don't look outside yourself for inspiration— look within.

Everyone makes mistakes.
Learn from yours and then move on.

I learn from my mistakes

When you get something wrong or let someone down, instead of beating yourself up, berating or criticising yourself learn what you can from the situation.

Own up to your mistake, apologise and make sure you don't make the same error again.

*You can't expect to feel good about yourself
if you focus on what is bad.*

I like the person I am

Everyone has things they like about themselves and things they wish they could ignore.

Instead of saying sorry for being someone that you're not, commit to being the best version of the person that you are.

*Don't let your feelings
stand in your way.*

I am moving forward

Before any triumph there is almost always a period of intense emotion but regardless of how you may feel in any given moment don't let these unhelpful feelings hold you back.

Instead, consider your most uncomfortable feelings as an essential rite of passage.

*Decide to live your best life
and then do whatever you need to do
to make it happen.*

I am committed to my goals

It's easy to talk about your goals without actually doing anything about them. But all the talk in the world won't get you very far.

Take one step towards your goal. Then take another and another and, before you know it, whatever it is that you want will be in sight.

*End each day with gratitude for today
and goodwill toward tomorrow.*

I express my gratitude

You don't have to be religious to give thanks at the end of each day.

Simply close your eyes, let your mind wander back over the day you've just had and take a minute to appreciate all the good that was in it.

Perfectionism
is the enemy of happiness.

I am happy with who I am

Seeking perfection is a vicious cycle.

When you don't feel you are good enough as you are, you try to be perfect. Perfection is impossible to achieve so you fail. Having failed, you don't feel so good about yourself … and on the downward spiral continues.

Choose to be happy with who you are and break this cycle once and for all.

There is a big difference
between a first-class effort and
a foolish level of effort.

I live a balanced life

If you want to live a happy and rewarding life you need to be smart about how you go about it.

Giving one part of your life all of your energy only to have nothing left for the rest of your life will leave you feeling depleted when the goal is to feel fulfilled.

Thinking you are better than someone else
will only make you feel good
until it starts to feel bad.

I am respectful

Although thinking you are better than someone might give your confidence a short-term boost, this will only last until you discover someone you think is better than you.

Instead of judging others (or yourself), be generous in your opinions and respect people for who they are.

Understand the risks,
but focus on your reward.

I focus on the outcome I want

There is nothing clever about being ignorant or naïve about a situation.

Being positive doesn't mean you shouldn't explore the negatives. Explore your options fully but once you know what could go wrong, focus all your efforts on what you want to go right.

Don't be afraid to be proud of who you are.
Authentic confidence is never boastful
or conceited.

I am proud of myself

One of the best ways to boost your
confidence is to make a list of your
achievements in life and the things you are
most proud of about yourself.

Keep this list close to your heart
and mind and call on it whenever your
confidence could do with a lift.

You don't need to go into battle with your fears.
They don't need to be defeated.
You just need to own up to them
and then let them go.

I make peace with my fears

Everyone experiences fear. It's a perfectly normal part of the human condition.

Instead of investing your energy in trying to conquer or overcome your fears, accept them. When you are honest about your fears they quickly lose the power they hold over you.

*Don't let your past
define your future.*

I learn from experience

Don't let the fact that something hasn't
worked or gone your way in the past put you
off trying again.

Know that the lessons you have learned
and the experience you have gained are
invaluable and will help you to achieve
your goal.

*Learn to love yourself
unconditionally.*

I release myself from perfection

There's no such thing as a perfect person.

Sometimes you will get things right and sometimes you won't. Sometimes things will go your way and sometimes they won't.

The key is to feel good about yourself regardless of the outcome.

The person you are,
right here, right now,
flaws and all is a worthwhile,
valuable and valid human being.

I am worth it

When you want to be the best you can be, it can be easy to get caught up creating a big long list of ways you can be even better.

Remind yourself that even if you never make a single change from this point forward, you are still deserving of a happy and fulfilling life.

There are no gold medals
to be won in the game of life.

I always have a good time

Life may be a game but there is a big difference between playing along and turning everything into a competition.

Instead of fighting for a place on the winner's dais, be a good sport. Show up, be supportive and above all make sure you enjoy it.

Enjoying the misfortune of others
is toxic to your self-esteem.

I am compassionate

Instead of criticising someone who is not doing as well as you are, imagine yourself in their shoes.

No two people are walking the same path in life. Don't judge someone who is not on your path.

*When you focus on what you want
you exponentially increase your chance
of getting it.*

I focus on my intentions

So many people spend all the time thinking about what they hope won't happen.

Rather than wasting your energy thinking about what might happen or what could happen instead focus your thoughts on what you want to happen.

*Change your thoughts
and your feelings will follow.*

I choose my thoughts

If you want to change the way you feel about something, start by changing the way you think about it.

Your thoughts will inform your feelings so decide how you want to feel, focus on thoughts that support this and watch your feelings fall into line.

Be brave.
Face your fears and then carry on regardless.

I have courage

Experiencing fear doesn't mean that you shouldn't do whatever it was you were wanting to do—it means it is important that you do it!

Get comfortable with the discomfort that fear brings and use it to fuel you as you work towards your goals.

*At any point you can decide
how you want the story of your future to be told.*

I let go of the past

If you have had a negative experience in the past learn what you can from it and then move on.

Lingering over past hurts, regrets or betrayals will leave you feeling bitter which is the last thing you need if you want your future to be sweet.

Forgive yourself
for what you have done
or have failed to do.

I forgive myself

Everyone makes mistakes and gets things wrong. It is not a sign of weakness; it's a sign of being human.

If you make a mistake or let someone down, apologise, make amends if you can and then forgive yourself. Holding on to guilt or remorse won't achieve anything except make you feel miserable for longer.

DOMONIQUE BERTOLUCCI

*Don't apologise for who you are
or criticise yourself for who you are not.*

I accept myself the way I am

While it's okay to apologise for things you've done (or failed to do), nothing erodes your self-confidence faster than constantly apologising for who you are.

The only time you really need to say sorry is when you hurt someone or let them down. The rest of the time you're doing nothing but hurting yourself.

You are good enough.
FACT.

I am good enough

When you want to be the best you can be, it's easy to fall into the habit of cataloguing your 'areas for improvement' and then using this list as a way to criticise or beat yourself up.

There is nothing wrong with wanting to improve yourself as long as you remember you are good enough just as you are.

Understand the difference
between humility and inferiority.
One will nurture your self-esteem
and the other will destroy it.

I embrace my gifts

While it's important not to be big-headed or boastful, hiding your light away won't serve you either.

Embrace your talents and gifts and enjoy the confidence that this knowledge brings.

You choose your experience.

I live a happy life

Regardless of what is going on in your life, you get to choose how you experience it.

If you want to live a happy life, focus on what is going well and pay as little attention as possible to the rest.

The fastest way to change your life
is to change the way you think about it.

I believe in my future

Before you try to create any changes in your life, examine the thoughts you have about them.

Remove any negative or critical thinking and reframe your thoughts so that they inspire, rather than undermine, the change you want to make.

One of the bravest things you can do is stand up for yourself and what you believe in.

I am interesting

If someone is telling you what they think, don't be afraid to disagree or share your opinion.

Having a different point of view doesn't make you argumentative. As long as you are respectful of other points of view it simply makes you interesting.

Taking responsibility
is about acting with courage and integrity.

I do the right thing

Taking responsibility isn't about blaming yourself; it's about maintaining your commitment to your values.

When you are responsible, you are honest when something feels wrong and you're not afraid to do what you can to put it right.

Stand up for yourself
and teach people how you want to be treated.

I respect myself

If someone puts you down, belittles you or attempts to diminish your confidence in some way, tell them to stop.

Whilst it might be easier in the moment to just 'put up with it', asking to be treated with respect is the best way to respect yourself.

*You are not broken
and you do not need to be fixed.*

I continue to grow

Everyone has flaws and imperfections.

There is nothing wrong with improving yourself but do it because you want to grow or change, not because there is something wrong with you if you don't.

You are not a share on the stock market; your value is not determined by your performance.

I value myself

Don't allow factors outside of yourself to determine how you see yourself.

It doesn't matter what you do, how small your dress size is or how big your bank balance is. What matters is that you value yourself for the person that you are.

*Being able to laugh at yourself
enhances your confidence.
Mocking yourself erodes it.*

I laugh with ease

When you make a mistake or mess
something up, instead of crying about it see
if you can find a way to laugh about it.

If you can find the humour in a situation,
at the very least, you'll be laughing through
your tears.

*Expect your life to be happy
and it will be.*

I look forward to my future

Your outlook affects the choices and the decisions you make.

When you believe you are going to have a good life, doing what it takes to make that your reality will feel like the most natural thing in the world.

If you want to achieve it,
you need to believe it.

I believe in my potential

If you want to make a change in your life, you need to do both the inner work and the outer work.

The effort you make to overcome your limiting beliefs and truly believe in your potential will be just as important to your success as planning your chosen course of action when it comes to making it happen.

*Don't be afraid
to ask for what you need.
You deserve it.*

I deserve it

Don't spend all of your time putting everyone else first only to put yourself last.

Your needs are no less important than anyone else's. Asking for what you want or need doesn't make you selfish, it makes you self-ist.

You need to be honest with yourself
if you want to create the future you deserve.

I own up to my dreams

So often people quietly harbour ideas about how they would like to improve or change their life without ever finding the courage to do something about it.

Be honest with yourself about what you want from your life. Once you declare this intent it will be much harder to hide from it.

If you want to be respected,
you need to ask for what you want
and explain exactly what you need.

I ask for what I need

Asking for what you want or need doesn't make you bossy or pushy, it makes you assertive.

Command respect by letting people know what you want and how you want to be treated—in a firm but pleasant way.

Think of self-improvement like
polishing a diamond.
You are already brilliant;
you just need to learn how to shine.

I allow myself to shine

Regardless of what it is you want from life, the biggest obstacle probably lies within you.

Remind yourself that you already are everything you need to be. You just need to learn how to let this very best version of you shine through.

As painful as it is,
it really doesn't matter if you fall down.
All that matters is how quickly
you can dust yourself off and get back up again.

I am strong

When something doesn't go your way, don't dwell on it or languish in disappointment.

While you don't need to ignore your setbacks to have a happy life, the less time you can spend agonising over them the better.

The fact that someone else has what you want is not cause for complaint. It is proof that it is possible and cause for celebration.

I am inspired

When someone else has what you want or has done what you want to do, it's easy to use it as an excuse to let go of your own motivation and commitment.

Rather than using this as an excuse to give up, use it as an inspiring reminder that you should *never* give up.

Don't allow your negative feelings
to hold the power in your life.

I own my feelings

Don't give your negative feelings any more power than they deserve.

Sometimes it will be helpful to explore them, other times it will be better to ignore them but, whatever you do, don't empower them or allow them to control your life.

If you want to do something differently,
you need to start by thinking about
it differently.

I see myself in the best possible light

When you are thinking about who you are and what you want, it's easy to focus on the negative—what is missing from your life and what you want to change about yourself.

Shift your perspective so that your attention is on all that you are and all that you already have.

While this won't change the facts, it will have an amazing impact on how you feel about them.

*Decide whose opinion matters
and stop worrying about everyone else.*

I know what is right for me

Don't waste your time seeking approval or hoping for positive feedback from anyone and everyone.

Instead, focus your energy on doing the thing that feels best to you. You can't please everybody all of the time so it's best not to even try.

When your desire for change is authentic,
you will have all the motivation you need.

I am motivated

Unless your goal is something you authentically desire you will never get very far with it.

If you are finding it hard to make the changes you want to make in your life, examine your motives more closely.

Find a driving factor you can really engage with and let go of all the 'shoulds' and 'coulds' in your life.

Confidence comes from within.
You can't find it in the eyes of someone else.

I nurture my self-esteem

Don't wait for someone or something else to make you feel good about yourself.

Boosting your self-confidence is not the responsibility of your partner, your job, your bank balance or your friends. Your self-esteem is your responsibility. Do what you need to do to keep it in good health.

If you strive for perfection you'll never be happy.
If you focus on being happy,
you won't care about being perfect.

I choose to be happy

You get to choose who you want to be and how you want to feel about yourself.

You can remain attached to perfectionist behaviour, constantly undermining your happiness and self-belief, or you can let go, focus on feeling good about yourself and stop worrying about everything else.

Life is not a battle to be won.
It is a journey to be experienced.

I enjoy the journey

In any rich and rewarding life there will always be ups and downs, peaks and troughs.

What matters isn't that you get an easy ride—it's that you stay in the saddle and enjoy the view from the road.

*Instead of comparing yourself
and finding yourself wanting,
count your blessings and remember
all that you have to be grateful for.*

I count my blessings

Focusing on all the ways you want to change or improve your life will quickly erode your self-confidence.

Before you make any plans for improvement take a minute to appreciate all the things in your life that are fine just as they are.

Decide what you want your future to be like,
then put your effort and your intentions
into making it your reality.

I honour my values

Don't just let life happen to you.

If you want to create a life that is happy and fulfilling to you, take the time to work out what matters most in your life.

Once you understand your values you can direct your efforts towards getting as much of them in your life as you can.

Don't let your failure in the past
get in the way of your success in the future.

I am successful

Don't let your past define your future. If something hasn't gone well for you or you feel like you have failed, it doesn't mean the same thing will happen next time.

Call on the wealth of knowledge and experience you have gained to give you an even greater chance of success next time.

When you do the right thing,
regardless of how you feel while doing it,
you will always feel good for having done it.

I act with integrity

It's not always easy to do the right thing.

But as hard as it can be, it is always better than doing the easy thing and then feeling bad about yourself for having done it.

Don't confuse your dreams and your fantasies.
A fantasy is something you enjoy
thinking about.
A dream is something you are willing to
do something about.

I enjoy my life

Don't confuse your fantasies with reality.

If there is something you want to change about your life, change it. But unless you are willing to take action, learn to accept things the way they are.

There's nothing wrong with having a fantasy life as long as it doesn't stop you from enjoying your real life.

Fall in love with yourself;
it's the best relationship you will ever have.

I am filled with love

Invest time and energy in building a wholehearted and healthy relationship with yourself.

Love yourself unconditionally and learn to treat yourself with the same kindness and respect you offer the other important people in your life.

Most strengths have a flip side.
Learn to accept yours.

I appreciate my flaws

When you find yourself focusing on one of your flaws or less than ideal qualities, actively seek out its flip side.

Every negative quality has a corresponding positive one so remind yourself how lucky you are to be flawed in this way.

Acknowledgements

My first thanks, as always, go to my wonderful agent, Tara Wynne at Curtis Brown, for her never-ending belief in my work. Thanks to Fran Berry, Rihana Ries, Marisa Wikramanayake and all the team at Hardie Grant for once again being such a delight to work with.

To my readers who connect with me on my Facebook page, thank you for sharing your experiences or simply stopping by to say hello. Hearing from you makes the solitary task of writing more than worthwhile.

I love my work and it is in no small part because of the people I get to share it with. To all my clients, past and present, the inspiring people who attend my workshops and those who sign up for my online programs, thank you for allowing me to be a part of your life.

To family and dearest friends, you've seen your names here before and I hope you know how important you are in my life.

A never-ending thank you to my mum and dad for their unconditional love and support.

To my darling Sophia and precious Toby, thank you for bringing so much love and laughter into my life. And to Paul, for everything, always.

About the Author

Domonique Bertolucci is the best-selling author of *The Happiness Code: 10 keys to being the best you can be* and the closely guarded secret behind some of the country's most successful people.

Passionate about getting the life you want *and* loving the life you've got, Domonique has a client list that reads like a who's who of CEOs and business identities, award-winning entrepreneurs and celebrities and her workshops and online courses are attended by people from all walks of life from all around the world.

Domonique helps her clients define their personal happiness prescription and then shows them exactly how to make it their reality.

Since writing her first book, *Your Best Life*, in 2006, Domonique has become Australia's most popular life strategist and happiness coach. More than ten million people have seen, read or heard her advice.

Domonique currently lives in London but her reach is truly global. In addition to her

Australian clients, she has coached people in London, Amsterdam, Paris, New York, Toronto, Singapore and Hong Kong. Her weekly newsletter *Love Your Life* has readers in more than sixty countries.

When she is not working, Domonique's favourite ways to spend her time are with her husband and two children, reading a good book and keeping up the great Italian tradition of feeding the people that you love.

Sign up for Domonique's free
course, *Life: make the most of yours*
domoniquebertolucci.com/life

Keep in touch with Domonique at:
domoniquebertolucci.com
facebook.com/domoniquebertolucci
twitter.com/fromDomonique
instagram.com/domoniquebertolucci

Other books by Domonique

The Happiness Code:
10 keys to being the best you can be

Love Your Life:
100 ways to start living the life you deserve

100 Days Happier:
Daily inspiration for life-long happiness

Less is More: 101 ways to simplify your life

The Kindness Pact: 8 promises to make you feel
good about who you are and the life you live

This edition published in 2017 by Hardie Grant Books,
an imprint of Hardie Grant Publishing
First published in 2016

Hardie Grant Books (Melbourne)
Building 1, 658 Church Street
Richmond, Victoria 3121

Hardie Grant Books (London)
5th & 6th Floor
52–54 Southwark Street
London SE1 1UN

hardiegrantbooks.com

A Cataloguing-in-Publication entry is available from
the catalogue of the National Library of Australia at
www.nla.gov.au

The Daily Promise: 100 ways to be kinder to yourself
978 1 74379 392 3

Cover design by Arielle Gamble
Typeset in Plantin Light 11/17pt by Kirby Jones

Printed in China by 1010 Printing International Limited